De

Deservingness

The Art of Getting More of What You Want

Tasha Chen

ISBN: 978-1-945446-70-2

To my son, Sebastian, who at twelve years old, wisely said, "Mom, I think you teach people to do more than manifest; I think you teach them how to deserve what they want first, because that's the only way they will get it."

Contents

Acknowledgments

This book began as an agreement between God and God, but it took many wonderful humans to bring it to life.

To every person who has participated in my life's journey, especially those who allowed me to see how little I believed I deserved—a genuine *thank-you!* The gift you led me to receive made it all worth it. I wish you love, joy, and your own deserving of the very best.

My loves, Natasha and Sebastian, whose lives are intertwined with mine—thanks for showing me unconditional love as you observed me doing the best I could.

My BFF Diane, my rock—without your belief in me, I wouldn't be capable of so much.

Readers of this book, we may or may never meet, yet knowing my story will have an impact on your life and lead you to the belief that you Deserve the Best. I know this will ultimately give you freedom from suffering, which was why I made the agreement with God in the first place to write this book! So, to you, a massive thank-you!

Introduction

This book is written by a woman who immediately experienced a worthiness wound at the very moment of her birth, then spent the next forty-plus years undoing it. It started with being denied financial support until it could be proven I was, indeed, my father's child, and this wound would weave the unhealthy pattern of needing to prove I deserved much of anything good from life.

In the end, it was a blessing as it led me to become *Deserving*.

But just how do you become Deserving?

How do you come to believe you should have it all?

On a conscious level, it makes logical sense for you to understand that you receive in life what you think you deserve. But there is not a lot of conversation about how one goes from: *I do not believe I deserve very much* to the opposite: *I think I deserve the best, or I am now operating from this new paradigm of believing I deserve the best*. So, this book was written for those of you who are tired of hearing you must believe you deserve the best in order to get it. Yet, you still do not know how to believe.

I have received enough slaps in the face in life to realize that I sure as heck did not think I deserved very much, which is my best credential for guiding you in transforming this belief. I wrote this book to share my own journey toward Deserving—the good, the bad the ugly, and everything in the process—with the hope that not another person has to live life as anything less than full because they are suffering from a painful belief that they do not deserve much.

I am a woman recovering from worthiness and Deservingness issues. My name is Tasha Chen, and for most of my life, I have suffered needlessly because I was missing one bit of information: the truth of what I deserved. I have endured pain, angst, and prolonged crying in my short lifetime, which was meant to be full of joy. I could regard my life as a wasted experience or as one to fill my heart with gratitude because I was given the opportunity to figure out what was required to put myself back on a lifepath leading to what I deserve: the best.

It took running away for my life to have my own come-to-Jesus moment. I call it my *come-to-Tasha moment* as I faced the reality of the lies I had believed for so long. I needed to look at my life directly and acknowledge that I was choosing all of it. Once I was willing to do that and cry out for help to end the patterns, everything changed. I embarked on a journey that started with me acknowledging the truth that I was living a life where I believed I deserved very little.

For two years, I did everything that came to my awareness for healing so I could be on this side to share the process, the journey, and my story with you. My heart's desire is that my openness and transparency in this book inspire you to give yourself the simple gift of being honest and transparent with yourself. Then, at the completion of reading this book, you will be committed to creating a new life, one where you can stand proudly next to me and say, "I deserve the best."

My intention is that this will not be just another self-help book. In the pages ahead, I hope you will feel my experiences and see yourself in my journey. I hope you will find the same courage I armed myself with so that I could get the thing I wanted the most: a wonderful romantic relationship as part of a life filled with peace, joy, and abundance.

Your struggle with Deservingness may be in your finances, in your health, or even how your family and friends treat you. As you read about my journey, my experience, and my process, be willing to try them on and, if nothing else, walk away from reading this book with, at a minimum, the willingness to ask yourself this question:

Am I living the life that is the best experience I can have?

If there is room for even the slightest opportunity for you to have more, then my guess is you do not yet believe you deserve more. Upon the completion of reading this book, I believe you will be willing to stand for everything you deserve.

Chapter One

Where It All Begins

Let's address the elephant in the room, the reason you picked up this book, why you may lie awake at night feeling inadequate and confused about your life. You don't have what you want in life because you don't think you deserve it. Period. End of story.

Besides my initial worthiness wound at birth, I have been involved in well over twenty relationships, and each involved extreme emotional suffering.

If anyone should know about Deservingness issues, it would be me.

Fact: It doesn't matter what you want in life; you won't get it or keep it if you don't believe you deserve it. Let's examine the link between Deservingness and consciously choosing experiences that create suffering and block what we all desire: genuine love, a happy life, and abundance.

Technically, you can have or create anything you desire in life. What good will that truth be if you do not know how to start believing you deserve it all so you can actually get it?

Here's the thing: I get it. I get you. I spent many nights with a pillow soaked in tears wondering how to get off this *merry-go-round to nowhere,* called My Life. My own life was showing me I had major Deservingness issues. For the longest time, I swore to myself to live by this life-changing quote:

> *You become what you believe – not what you wish or want, but what you truly believe. Wherever you are in life, look at your beliefs. They put you there.*
>
> ~ Oprah

I preached that quote like a Baptist minister on a revival Sunday until my own messed up, recurring patterns made it dawn on me there was something missing. *It wasn't about what I believed at all.* Sure, I believed I could be rich, and I believed I could have a great guy in a happy and healthy relationship. I believed I was a good person, I believed in God, and that I could have all the wonderful gifts to be had in life.

Did I believe I *deserved* most of those things? No!

What I really believed I deserved was:

- I had to work for the success.
- I had to suffer first to find love.

- God would only consider blessing me when I had duly begged forgiveness.

The truth is I never believed I deserved the good, wonderful, happy stuff to come easily for me.

MY COME-TO-JESUS MOMENT

I am sharing this come-to-Jesus moment because I believe there are other women, and people in general, who have all the intellectual tools but still find themselves suffering and are not quite sure why. I consider myself smart, intelligent, and successful, and results in my life reflect this to be true. So, it was surprising to find myself in a three-year emotionally abusive and traumatic relationship when I should have known better.

The idea that I was limiting myself because I did not believe I deserved better was so foreign to me, so alien, my brain immediately responded: *Does not compute. Does not compute. Do not understand. What?* I always thought what I wished for, intended, or desired was what I was receiving in life. Introducing my mind to Deservingness helped me understand what this concept truly meant; clearly what I felt I deserved was causing me pain.

My Three-Year Denial Period

Like a lot of women, my number-one goal in the area of relationships has always been to be in a loving, happy, healthy, romantic, love-of-my-life-type relationship. When my marriage of thirteen years failed, I found myself even more committed to that quest and became involved in a new relationship that lasted three years.

For that entire period, I would convince myself every day this man was, in fact, the one I should let love me. I believed I could right all my previous relationship wrongs if I just did everything *right* with him, whatever it took to make the relationship work.

For three years, I denied that I was in trauma, that I was being emotionally abused, that I was being lied to, that I was being hurt, and everything in between. Instead, I simply tried harder and harder every single day to reach the result I wanted, which was a happy and romantic relationship—something that would never arrive.

I recall being asked by my coach, "What is the longest period you have gone in this relationship without crying?"

I answered, "Two days."

He said, "Tasha, that is suffering; that is not a relationship."

Face-to-Face With the Truth

Having endured this traumatic relationship for three years, I would say to myself: *Okay, so your guy is a liar. That is okay. You love him.*

I went about my life in this manner until the day of our third anniversary. We were scheduled to go out to celebrate. But then, he told another lie—not much different from any of the others, not really a big deal of a lie. However, on that particular day, I wasn't in the mood for silly lies.

I have always had an internal voice that says: *I will give a guy three years.*

As luck would have it, this lie struck a chord when I needed it to strike. I remember driving home that afternoon, knowing we would see each other soon to start the celebration of our anniversary, and I remember driving past the cane fields of Belle Glade with nothing to do but think.

In this truth moment, I had to ask myself: *Tasha, you are with a liar. Are you okay with that?*

And finally, the answer was *no.*

The Big Question

This revelation set in motion a sequence of events that led me to flee the country the next morning. It was the strangest thing. Once I acknowledged I was being lied to and abused, a powerful instinct kicked in that screamed: *RUN FOR YOUR LIFE!*

I rushed home, and in five minutes flat, I had a suitcase packed and the last-minute thought to grab my passport as I ran out the door. I was panicked, and I remember trying to figure out why. My intuition kept pushing me to get away from the house before he arrived. I suppose three years of breaking up and making up a hundred times had taught me that if I stayed until he arrived, I would simply be back in the noose of his deception and control.

As my car drove itself south on I-95 that day, I watched the raindrops fall off my windshield while my mind tried to figure out where to go for safety and what to do next. I pulled over and decided to call my good friend Lisa, who ran a luxury fishing vacation business.

My instructions to her were simple: "Lisa, I need you to book me on a flight to anywhere leaving from Fort Lauderdale airport tomorrow morning, and find me a place to stay for a week when I get there."

She's the kind of matter-of-fact friend who simply said, "Do you have a passport and a credit card?"

Once we agreed I would send her pictures of both, she hung up the phone to take care of the details.

Of course, my phone was going off nonstop with alerts of phone calls and text messages from my boyfriend. He was angry because I wasn't being responsive so he didn't know what was going on with me. We spoke briefly that night, and I admitted I was in Fort Lauderdale.

"No problem," he said, "I'll come meet you."

The conversation finally unraveled to the point where he was forced to face the fact I wasn't going to meet him, I really was not home, and, no, I wasn't with some other man cheating on him. I simply did not want to be with him.

I barely slept that night. I had found the last overpriced room in the city, and after double bolting the doors, I mostly laid wide awake with the phone right next to me—just in case I needed to call 911. The next morning, after receiving my airline and flight details from Lisa, I boarded a ten o'clock flight headed to San Juan, Costa Rica.

The boyfriend tried again on the phone, going back and forth between bargaining with me to stay and threatening me that if I left, our relationship was over. When the doors to our flight finally closed, I called my best friend and burst into the most intense tears of relief: *I had gotten away from him.*

But it wasn't over. Once I landed and made it through customs, I was greeted by a teenage kid holding a sign with my name spelled incorrectly. Since no one, including me, knew where the next leg of my journey was to be, I assumed he had been sent by Lisa to direct me. I was right. He took me to the small local airline that would fly me over to the peninsula. After check-in, I had hours to spare, so we sat together for lunch, and he allowed me to use his hot spot for Wi-Fi access.

As soon as I was connected, messages and missed calls from the boyfriend came reeling in like rapid fire. I ignored them all to send Lisa a message letting her know I had arrived and all was well. We had a few exchanges about the next leg of my trip before I had to stop texting her to take a closer look at the nasty messages my boyfriend was sending me.

> *You Bitch, You Whore, you better answer your phone, or you will not have a house to come back to. I know what you did, I know you are with _____ (the name of the teenage kid who had just come to greet me) and that you are checked in at Sansa. If you don't answer your phone, I will be showing up at Crocodile Bay (the resort Lisa had only a few seconds ago informed me I would be staying at) tonight!*

I stared at my phone, moving back and forth between shock and fear. The blood drained from my face, and my heart raced so fast I began having palpitations. I felt like I was in a thriller, and the bad guy had satellites all over the world, tracking my every move. The instinct to run for my life was back again, but faced with the realization that he had all the information of what I was to do next, I stood frozen on the side of the road, shaking uncontrollably. The teenage boy looked at me as if he had no clue what was going on but wanted to get as far away from me as he could.

Two hours later, I finally pieced it all together. He had tapped my phone. He was reading all the messages I was receiving. He had also called Lisa in the meantime (after getting her number from my phone) and tried to convince her to book him the same itinerary as me because he wanted to surprise me.

Thank goodness, she had the wisdom to say, "I think she just wants some alone time."

The story worsens. With all that time on my hands before my flight was due to leave, I sat and looked back at so many coincidences: things he would mention—telling me he could read my mind, randomly asking to check my phone just by chance after I had received a message from an old boyfriend. It was clear he had tapped my phone for the entire three years of our relationship.

That night, I had no choice but to ask God out loud, "Why is this happening to me?"

This was my come-to-Jesus moment.

I continued, "What have I done to deserve this? How is this my life?"

Even though there was no burning bush, no parting clouds, and no thunder rolling, I heard the quiet and resolute voice of God speaking as clear as day in the pit of my soul, "Because you do not believe you deserve any more than this, Tasha."

WHERE ARE YOU NOW?

> *Even if the cause of your suffering dies, you will just replace it with another person to make you suffer. Until you change the program. Knowledge is power, but knowledge about yourself is self-empowerment.*
>
> ~ Dr. Joe Dispenza

Self-evaluation is a major requirement in ending any suffering or pain you may be enduring. While we can choose, consciously or unconsciously, to continue to suffer, we also have the choice of looking at ourselves and seeing the truth of our reality. This part of the process is key in achieving the peace I believe you desire and deserve.

When you are able to know firsthand why you experience life and relationships the way you do, you become self-empowered. You hold the key to changing everything in your life. The best gift is to be true to yourself, to call yourself out on your stuff, and to be willing to unlock the prison you have put yourself in.

Taking Stock in Your Life

Calling yourself out will require a level of honesty you might never have had with yourself; however, it is a crucial first step in recognizing what you believe you deserve. As you begin, I encourage you to look at all areas of your life. If any part of your life feels less than ideal, put it under the microscope as you read through this book. The area does not need to be chaotic; it just needs to be less than ideal.

You know intuitively if you want more for yourself in that area of your life than you are currently experiencing right now. I encourage you to evaluate this piece of your life, especially if it causes you to suffer in any way—feeling inadequacy, pain, or hurt. Really analyze or assess what is going on in those areas and ask: *why*?

For example, my relationship was far less than ideal, but I stayed. I stayed for three years. I had to ask why I did that and what was not ideal about it. I had to be brutally honest with myself in a way I would never do with my friend because I would be too embarrassed, ashamed, self-critical, or fearful that she would criticize me.

But when I went through the process of being honest with myself, I looked at the facts. My relationship was causing me to suffer every day and staying was a clear sign I didn't believe I deserved better.

So, I encourage you to look at all the areas of your life. If anyone feels less than ideal, have a come-to-*you* moment and be truthful with yourself about what is less than ideal. Examine what is involved and why it is less than ideal.

Are You Ready to Be Free?

This may seem like a rhetorical question, but the reality is, sick as it may sound, Deserving very little may have become such a norm for you that you are scared to change or even believe you can. Having lived a prisoner to your past for so long, you are now faced with a choice. You can continue to have the past rule and punish you in life, or you can decide you are ready to be free of it.

Your past may say you don't deserve very much, and your present may agree. To create a future that reflects you deserve the best, you must learn to look at the past as a gift and free yourself from the burden of experiences that cause you to continue to suffer and be in pain. Every moment you continue to stay in pain, not fully enjoying your life, means you are choosing to remain a prisoner to your past.

The person who believes they deserve the best has first done the work of releasing the grip of their past.

THE LIES THAT BIND YOU

On your journey to Deservingness, you will be traveling from living lies you have believed, lived by, and told yourself, and arriving at the new destination of fully owning The Truth. This journey will create a new way of life, new beliefs, new actions, and a new you. Your location in The *Lie* is what keeps you disconnected from The Truth.

The goal is reconnection, to realign and get back to who you really are—who you have always been—and to The Truth. The Truth is you deserve to be loved, you deserve to be happy, you deserve abundance, and you deserve to experience joy. You deserve to be reconnected to the true you.

I want to show you how to heal your fractured parts that have separated you from perfection by your past choices, which were based on your beliefs about yourself.

What Is the Truth?

In order to understand and appreciate the truth, you must shine light on The Lie.

The Lie for me had many voices:

- I was a sinner.
- I was wrong.
- I was bad.
- I was guilty.
- I was promiscuous.
- I deserved to suffer.
- I was unloved by God.
- I was unlovable.
- I was unworthy of what I was seeking.

Can you relate?

This set of beliefs is a lie—*The Lie*. You cannot acknowledge The Truth without first acknowledging The Lie you have been telling yourself, believing, acting from, and using as grounds for accepting bad life situations.

The Truth is:

- You were born whole and complete.
- You are love.
- You are loved.

The Truth is that no matter what you have done, where you have been, who you have been with, or what you have said, nothing in your life separates you from the perfection of how you were created. Nothing you could have done or will ever do will separate God's love from you. There is nothing you need to do, to become, or to stop doing. Nothing.

Just as you are, God loves you. And that is *The Truth.*

Agree to It

Reflect on all you acknowledge as less than ideal in your life, all that has put you on this path of feeling unworthy and undeserving and caused you to experience suffering and pain. You were never intended to experience any of these negative things. It was never part of your makeup. You were, however, given free will, but by believing The Lie, you chose these experiences as evidence that The Lie was, in fact, The Truth.

So, the hardest pill to swallow on this journey to Deservingness might be that you have to review your life, take responsibility, and acknowledge you agreed to all of it. As everything was occurring, before it happened, and as you were in the process, you were continuously—over and over—saying yes to the pain, yes to the suffering, yes to people treating you less than valuable, yes to it all. You agreed to it.

The good news is you can end that agreement.

Believing You Deserve the Best

I stand as a living witness that embracing The Truth of who you are, what you deserve, what you are worthy of, what you were brought here for, is your true life's purpose. Until you accomplish that major goal of knowing you deserve the best, you will wander through life like the eagle among the yard chickens, fighting for scraps, not knowing its true ability to rule the sky.

What is the journey toward Deserving like?

Imagine you go back into your mother's womb and come out as a new you, in essence, dying to The Lie that said you ever deserved anything less than the very best. This is the journey I am describing.

Right now, you do not need to believe it is possible to transform and become a new version of yourself. The only thing needed in this moment is your willingness to acknowledge in your heart of hearts that you desire a life in which you see a different, happier, more fulfilled, and joyous version of yourself.

Chapter Two

You're In Relationship With Everything

You are in relationship with everything. Understanding what we believe we deserve can be a little tricky because, on the surface, we all think we deserve the best. We walk around with big promotional signs that say: *Bring me all the great things in life because I think I should have it.*

The only way to know what you truly believe you deserve will be to observe:

- How you relate to yourself
- How you relate to others
- How others relate to you
- How you experience major areas in life, such as money, quality of life, and health

YOUR RELATIONSHIP WITH YOU

Did you know your very first relationship is the one you have with yourself? This relationship mirrors everything else you experience in life. In order to understand how you receive what you deserve, you must first have a complete understanding of your relationship with you.

So let's begin looking at this relationship. I have become a master at looking at the relationship I had with myself to discover what I really believed I deserved. What I realized is I thought little of myself and life was continuously saying: *Yes, here you go; here is proof you deserve very little.*

What Do You Think About You?

This is possibly the most profound question you will ever be asked in your lifetime.

What do you think about you?

Take a few moments to answer these questions:

- What do you think about how loveable you are?
- What do you think about the qualities you have?
- What do you think about your abilities?
- What do you think about the way you show up in relationships?
- What do you think you should or should not have in life?
- What do you think about how easy life should be?

- What you think about whether you are good or bad?

Who Told You About Yourself?

As you begin to see how you think about yourself, be reminded of The Truth. You came into this life experience pure, complete, and whole. I dare say *flawless*. You were never a sinner; you were never wrong. In this lifetime, nothing about you needed to be fixed or healed. You were never broken. Most of what you think about yourself has been *put on you* by others.

At six or seven years old, I walked into a bedroom where both my parents lay covered under the sheets; it is the only memory I have of seeing my parents together. Since it was such a rare occurrence, I remember walking into that room and sheepishly looking at them with the innocent eyes of a kid so happy to see her parents together. Even more so, I longed to be in that bed, snuggled up with them.

I stood there for a long time. All I wanted was for them to say something loving to me and offer me an invitation to join them. But neither of those desires were met. My parents were acting strange, but I didn't understand what it was about. All I know is that day I decided I was unwanted and unlovable, because surely if the two people meant to want and love me the most couldn't even include me in their own moment of *love,* then this was the truth about me: *I was unlovable.*

Those beliefs would stay with me for forty additional years. Can you imagine forty years with all the life experiences I attracted to prove just how unloved and unwanted I really was? At forty-six years old, when I finally looked back at this scene with adult eyes, I realized I had caught my parents in an intimate moment. There were so many other layers to what I saw in that scene that could not have been understood by a child. None of those layers contained their belief that I was unwanted or unlovable. I had believed a lie about myself for a long, long time.

How about you?

What life experiences have you allowed to create beliefs about yourself and what you deserve?

What have others told you about you?

Make a list of all you have come to believe about yourself and note whether each belief was told to you or created by an experience you had. Begin to dissect each one a little further. You will see The Truth; they all began with what others said, and you agreed they were true.

At this moment, if I called you another name besides your given name, you would correct me, right?

If I insisted I had used your true name, nothing I said could convince you otherwise—especially if I said this is what I believe your name is, what I think it should be.

You would stand firmly, letting me know your true name, correct?

It's the same with all the things others have said about you. Maybe when you were younger, you thought others knew the truth about you so you accepted their statements. Now, you no longer have to accept what they think. You decide what's true for you.

It's time to look at all the beliefs you wrote down and ask this question: *Is it true?*

- Did someone call you a sinner? Is it true?
- Did someone say you are a bad person? Is it true?
- Did someone tell you that you are incapable of succeeding in life? Is it true?

Question everything everyone has said about you with the qualifying measurement: *Is this true about me?*

After years of suffering, languishing between the erroneous thoughts I had of myself and the ones I inherited by way of others' opinions, I finally had had enough. I had suffered enough. I had stayed in my patterns long enough. I had hurt myself and others long enough. It was time. I wanted to be done with the perception of myself I was living under.

When I finally decided I had the power to create anything in my life, I chose what the ideal me looked like, the me I wanted to believe in and could now live by. As you are on your journey to becoming Deserving, let's begin thinking about an ideal you.

What would you want to walk around thinking as The Truth about yourself?

YOUR RELATIONSHIP WITH OTHERS

Ever played the blame game?

You know the one, where you make every person in your life responsible for the experiences you are having with them?

I have done that quite a lot. I have made everyone the bad guy who hurt me. Naturally, I became the victim.

What you experience with others is only a mirror effect of the relationship you have with yourself. So, in order to become Deserving, you need to examine first your relationship with yourself and then the deeper clues from your relationships with others.

When you think of those in your life who caused you emotional pain, you may be tempted to become angry, frustrated, hateful, or resentful toward these people. Remember, you need to take responsibility for the fact they showed up and allowed you to see what you believed you deserved at that time.

What They Think You Deserve

If you have ever been really angry at someone being disrespectful to you, hurting you, being inconsiderate or harmful to you in any way, you simply experienced that person telling you what you believed you deserved from them. This Truth brought me such peace.

I remember coming to the realization that every person in my life, especially lovers, could only treat me in the way I communicated to them that I deserved to be treated. If I wanted to be treated any differently, I had to first believe I deserved it. Naturally, they would then have no choice but to honor how I believed I deserved to be treated.

So here is an activity for you: Document how you think the important people in your life treat you, speak to you, honor you. If you want to know what they think you deserve, this will be the most eye-opening exercise you will ever do. When you are complete, what you will have written is what you have told all of these people you believe you deserve from them.

When I accepted three years of lying and emotional abuse, it was me, saying to my partner: *Yes, I believe it's okay for you to behave in this way because this is all I think I deserve.* It's a tough pill to swallow when you take that level of responsibility, but it's the kind of bitter medicine that wakes you up and makes you want to change.

The Rating System

Do you now understand others treat you as you have instructed them to do, based on what you believe you deserve?

Imagine yourself at the center of your life and considering your relationships with others. Here is a simple rating system for viewing the significant people in your life. As you increase your level of Deservingness, this will be a great system for helping you as you relate to the people in your life.

There are three categories:

1. Your lovers
2. Your believers
3. Your teachers

Your lovers mirror the part of you that is loving, deserving, gracious, and kind. You want to prioritize these people and give them your time and attention.

They know your truth, and they love you anyway. If you have believed for a long time that you are not deserving of love and people treating you well, it may be difficult to receive their love or even spend time with them—make yourself do it anyway.

Then there are your believers. They only see your light. They see the best in you. They believe in you. Show up for them because they remind you of parts of yourself, the parts you do not always value. Honor them and give your best to them.

The last category includes your teachers. It hurts to be with them. They show you all you do not love about yourself—how little you believe you deserve. Take the lessons quickly and work on them. You are meant to learn from them, not stay with them.

Make a list of the top ten relationships in your life, putting each person in one of these three categories. If you are in a business that serves others, your clients would be listed as one person or group, and they would be listed as believers.

Your People

As you learn to become more Deserving, life will bring you people to fill the rating system. Once it becomes clear what you show people you deserve, your job will be to continuously shift and sort, knowing all your people are showing up to move you forward as you heal The Lie and commit to becoming Deserving. Consider that all who show up in your life are your people. They have been sent to help you understand how to use the rating system until you master it.

YOUR RELATIONSHIP WITH THINGS YOU DESIRE

We have concluded that you are in relationship with everything you experience in your life. We have looked at your relationship with yourself and your relationship with others. Now let's look at physical objects and experiences you desire to have in life.

Specifically, I am going to choose the top three:

- Money
- Success
- Ease or quality of life

Let's look at your relationship with these three things. Consider the experiences that keep you awake at night, taking away your joy or robbing you of peacefulness. Instead of using your energy to worry about why these things are not working out the way you would like, use that time and energy to be truthful with yourself, asking yourself what you believe you deserve in each area.

Do you truly believe you deserve what you are asking for?

What You Don't Have

For a long time, I wished with all my heart that I could have the highest level of success I could achieve. I wanted a lot of money, so I could spend the majority of my days on the beach. I wished really hard for all this success. Then, the day arrived when I realized I was wishing in vain because I did not believe I deserved it.

So, let's look at you. What don't you have? How does it make you feel?

Let's think about money. When it comes to your financial reality and the financial abundance you desire, bring your awareness to how much you do not have in that area. What do you lack?

When it comes to success, do the same. How much success have you not yet achieved?

When it comes to enjoying a quality lifestyle, what are you not experiencing?

Once you have outlined what you do not have, take some time to understand how it makes you feel. I can guess with 100 percent certainty you are going to be hard on yourself and feel unaccomplished—pretty much like crap. Look back at your list and remember my story.

Have you been wishing for these things without truly believing you deserve them?

If you are not experiencing what you desire, remember, you are in relationship with these things. They are reflecting what you believe you deserve or do *not* believe you deserve.

What Are You Attracting?

If you want to see the writing on the wall about what you believe you deserve, life is showing it to you. It is showing you in the way you attract what you desire.

Ask yourself these questions about money:

- *How am I attracting money?*
- *Is it coming in small amounts?*
- *Is it hard for me to receive money?*
- *Is it difficult to earn it?*
- *Am I constantly struggling to make more?*

The answers are your *attraction field*. This field attracts what you believe you deserve and determines your experience of money in your life. If you want a different experience with money, you must work on believing you deserve that different experience.

You Can Change Your Reality

The thing I love the most about this work is the simplicity with which we can begin to change our reality. I would like to invite you to consider becoming the person who receives the things you desire in life from a place of Deserving the best.

Take a few minutes to imagine how different your life might be if you woke up every day with the thought: *I deserve the best,* and that truth came as naturally to you as breathing.

What thoughts would you think about yourself as you went through the day?

Consider the people you spend the most time with. How differently might they be interacting with you?

And since you deserve the best, life would be easy-breezy. How does that feel to you?

When I imagined myself as that new Deserving person, I became relentless in my pursuit to be that woman. I wanted to feel that way about myself and my life so badly, I became ultra-committed to doing whatever was required to get there.

Do you want to become the person you just imagined so that things and experiences come to you with ease, grace, and consistency, with the flow that makes your heart sing?

Then, the first simple step is to declare out loud for the Universe to hear:

I deserve the best!

Chapter Three

Why Am I Here?

THE THINKING THAT BROUGHT YOU HERE

When you are suffering and living your life in a way that reflects the little you believe you deserve, you want to understand:

- *Why am I here?*
- *Why am I in this experience?*
- *Why is this happening to me?*

Why, why, why.

It is a desperate need to understand all the moving parts that came together so that you, with what can feel like all the misfortune in the world, could create the life circumstances that would cause you suffering and pain. I am here to say the reason you are in this life experience is because you thought yourself into it.

The most empowering part of this journey is realizing how fully in control we really are. I know what it is like to feel as if your entire existence, your entire experience of life is at the mercy of everyone else. However, realize you are at the center of your life experience: you are the cause of everything you experience, you are making the agreements, you are believing The Lie.

Once you acknowledge The Truth, the next step is easy. You can simply move forward by choosing to think a new thought—a thought that will create a reality you enjoy.

The Gift of Your Past

The past holds the lessons, and the future is where you change it.
~ Author unknown

I have found that many people like me, who are addicted to suffering and pain, use the past to continue to hurt themselves even more by focusing on mistakes and wrong choices they have made, things they cannot forgive themselves for. The past becomes a burdensome aspect of their life, used repeatedly as a self-beating tool each and every day.

On my journey to understanding Deservingness and coming to a place of peace and happiness, I switched from thinking of the past as this bad, evil thing to thinking of it as a gift that could inform me and help me understand what I deserve. Then, like alchemy, the process took me from being a prisoner to being free. It showed me how I could go from living from a lack of Deservingness to becoming Deserving.

Once I could understand the gift present in past experiences, that gift became the catalyst for new decisions, new choices, new behaviors, and new actions because I could clearly look back and see what I accepted or chose before. I could also see the results those previous decisions brought.

If I want a new result, I look for the lesson from the past to tell me when I need to act differently.

Stop and Think

As I looked back over my own life experience—one after another failed relationship, one after another disappointment, and hurt and pain from childhood experiences—I realized I was constantly in reaction mode to what life was serving up for me. I was always conducting this after-the-fact review of experiences life was giving me.

I never stopped and thought about why I experienced this continued stream of unpleasantness in the first place. Perhaps, this was one of my biggest *ah-has* on the journey to Deservingness. One day, I finally stopped and gave myself enough time to think. I asked myself what was at the center of all these experiences. What was it about me that made me so unfortunate enough to bring into my life experiences all these unpleasantries?

Instead of reacting and responding to all these happenings, I finally stopped long enough to think about what created them in the first place. If you are in a pattern of self-destruction, acting from a place of Deserving very little, stop and examine your life and think about it long enough to see all the moving parts, all the pieces coming together. This reflection is a major step; spend the time to understand what is in the middle of the entire picture. Only then will you see it is *you*, and something about you, who is creating it all.

Your Inner Story

As you start the self-exploratory process, you will find there are literally some experiences you signed up for, said yes to experiencing in your life. I call those agreements.

Agreements might look or sound like:

- *I think life should be hard.*
- *I think I should suffer.*
- *I think I should be treated poorly in relationships.*

When you stop long enough to examine your life and return to the root cause of all your experiences, you will find you had a thought that made you agree to all of it. Your thoughts led you to make agreements about how you should experience life, and then, based on those agreements, life fulfilled the contract. It gave you exactly what you said yes to.

> *Man is a thinking center, and can originate thought. All the forms that man fashions with his hands [or all life experiences we create, including being treated poorly] must first exist in this thought; he cannot shape a thing [or have an experience] until he has thought that thing.*
>
> ~ Wallace D. Wattles
> *The Science of Getting Rich*

On your path to understanding what you deserve, you will need to take a deep dive into what thoughts—about yourself and about life—are creating what you think you deserve. Leave no stone uncovered.

Look at every area of your life:

- The way you experience your relationships
- The way you experience financial abundance
- The way you experience your health
- The way you feel connected to God
- The way you are able to treat yourself to the things you desire

View every area of your life through the looking glass of this question: *What thoughts create the story I tell myself that, in turn, leads to how I experience this area of my life?*

Thinking Lies

Once you have uncovered your inner story, you will have made the most startling discovery. Without a shadow of a doubt, you will see you have agreed to a lot of lies about yourself. At first you may feel confronted, and it may be difficult to accept this reality once you realize your agreements caused it. You might become angry at your parents, your family, your church, your elders, your friends, or anyone whose stories brought you here.

But let's talk about solutions. Once you turn on the light of awareness, you already have 80 or 90 percent of the solution. Sure, you may have agreed to all these lies. Nobody truly wants to agree to living a life of Deserving very little, of suffering and struggles, and of being treated poorly. Nobody wants to agree to that.

Somewhere in your makeup and life experience there have been thoughts you allowed to become agreements, and those agreements then shaped your life. Now that the light switch is on and you are seeing life for what it is, the next step is to acknowledge these old thoughts were all lies. They are not The Truth; they are not your truth, and you now have a choice in making a new agreement.

Take your power back and ask yourself: *What do I want to think about myself?*

One day I realized that for three years I had made an agreement, a thought, that said it was okay for me to be in love with a liar. Once I realized I had literally and consciously agreed to that reality, I beat myself up badly. I spent a lot of time asking why, why, why.

I am smarter than this. I know better. I have all of the things I need in life. I do not need to put myself in this situation.

Then it finally hit me: I do not want to agree to this thought anymore because it causes me pain. It causes me to have a less-than-ideal relationship. I simply stopped for long enough to ask myself what I wanted to agree to regarding how I experience someone in a relationship.

I got to the place where I simply asked myself: *What is a new thought you want to think, Tasha? What will be the new story you tell yourself? What agreement do you want to make?*

The simple answer was: *I want to agree that the person I am in a relationship with is living in full integrity.*

This led to the new story: *Tasha, you deserve to be in a relationship with a person who will be honest with you.*

PATTERNS THAT KEEP YOU EMPTY

Figuring things out can be simple. In my own experience, there were a repeated set of life experiences that, when reviewed, showed me how I had chosen to go through life. These patterns were repeated experiences—the same experience with different persons, different faces, different times—but always with the same pattern.

If you can identify a pattern, you can solve your own problems.

Here is the great news: Yes, we have turned on the light to your patterns and your addictions. I know it was not the most amazing experience you have ever had in your life.

Now that you know this, you can't return to not knowing it.

From this moment forward, you will always be aware of the choices you are making to either continue in the pattern or to choose differently. That awareness alone is your ticket to freedom. Moment by moment, knowing you are making a choice is the freedom you have always longed for. Breaking the patterns by practice, self-control, and self-mastery will take you directly to the life that you truly deserve and desire.

What Are You Addicted To?

I had been two years into my dysfunctional and emotionally traumatic relationship in which every two days were a complete emotional meltdown. One day, I called my best friend and excitedly told her on the phone that I had finally figured it out. I had figured out what my problem was, and I was so excited to share it with her.

On the other end was my friend who had suffered maybe even more than I had because she had watched me go through this pain every day for two years—every single day in suffering and pain, putting myself down, being put down, being emotionally abused. She was excited to know I had figured out what was going on.

I said to her, "I figured it out. I am addicted to suffering."

Man, was she excited. "Finally, Tasha. You got it and this will end. You will end the suffering, and I will end the suffering. And we can move on and create the happy life that we both know you deserve."

Except, that is not what happened. Just because you know what you're addicted to doesn't mean anything has changed. It would take me another year after identifying my addiction to do something about it.

As you start exploring your patterns, you realize there has been a reward, a sort of pleasure, that you have been receiving from the unpleasant experiences of your life. As strange as that might sound, there is a reward in it for you, and if you are willing to look at what that reward might be—whether it comes out sounding great or not—you can solve your problem.

When I evaluated the pattern I had in relationships, I had moments of feeling in love, moments of feeling sad, the euphoria of being treated like a queen, and the crappy feeling of someone not showing up for me. But the thing that was constant in that pattern was how much suffering I endured.

What exactly is the pattern that keeps repeating for you?

What is the feeling, the emotion, the one constant you can identify as the reward you are receiving from this pattern?

That one constant is your addiction.

My addiction started with this thought: *Love = Suffering*. So, every time I felt *in-love,* I would also create the circumstances that would lead me to suffering. Being right about this thought was my sick and sad reward.

Your Own Movie

Let's be real. Examining your patterns is not the most fun exercise I could ever give you to do. I know because I have had to do it. As I went through painful relationships, one after the other, it never once occurred to me that I was in a pattern. I am talking about thirty-plus years. I was having the same experience over and over, and it never entered my conscious thought at all.

I know if you are suffering and have not yet solved the mystery, you are also probably not aware that you are in a pattern. So, sit back, close your eyes, and travel back through your life. Since you identified your patterns in the last section, sit back, and now watch yourself in these patterns as if you are watching a movie.

For me, this was the biggest eye-opener, the biggest self-realization I probably ever experienced in my life. Finally, I was not a third party telling someone about what was happening. I was watching myself, time after time, *choose* to suffer. I was watching myself choose the life experiences that would give me my rush, my addiction, my suffering kick.

Once I did that, I could not turn my inner TV off. I could no longer lie to myself. I had, in fact, gone through all those experiences. More importantly, I had chosen each and every one.

I dare say that watching your own movie, watching yourself in your life, is going to give you more information about you than any other personal development journey. Once you see it for yourself, you are fully aware of what you are doing and why you are doing it. The light switch is on.

Is It Worth It?

Eventually you will come to the point in your movie when you are in the present. You will have felt all the feelings, experienced all the emotions, beat yourself up, and most likely, looked back with regret. You will have gone through the entire emotional range and brought yourself to the current day. Reviewing the movie, you now have an important question to ask.

Has it been worth it?

Consider the addiction you agreed to and the rush of having that addictive experience over and over again. The answer is simply yes or no.

Is it worth it to you?

When I watched the movie of my life, I saw the time away from my kids that suffering caused me, the lack of joy, the lack of peace, the soulful yearning, the spirit dampening, the extra energy it took just to live and breathe, the way I felt less-than in several relationships, and the unfulfillment of my heart's desires. None of that was worth continuing to choose this pattern for myself.

Only I could answer that question for myself. There were clearly many times when I was not aware I was in a pattern. I was not aware I was addicted to suffering, but now that I was aware, it seemed natural to ask: *Is this worth it or not?*

I ask that question of you, after you have watched your movie. What has this lack of Deservingness caused you to experience in life, and is it worth it to you to continue experiencing it?

WITHOUT A VISION, YOU PERISH

How about we create your new movie? If you feel like you have no idea where to begin, no worries, I understand.

I still remember the first time I became aware of the idea that I was receiving in life what I believed I deserved, not what I was wishing or intending. Once I had that awareness, the next thing I had to acknowledge was I had no idea what it looked like to deserve anything else. I had no vision of what that might be like; I had no experiences to draw upon.

I had certainly never seen other options in any of my life experiences, so I drew a blank. I could not create this new reality because I had no way of seeing it. It might be the same for you. Without a vision of what it looks like to be Deserving your best, your chances of experiencing it or manifesting it will be slim to none. So, let's talk about what it looks like to have a vision of what you deserve.

Have fun with this. You have suffered long enough. You have endured life experiences that were never yours to have. You have lived with the trauma for too long. It is time to take your power back and create the reality you would love to experience and then experience it. Remember, as Author Rashawn Renee says, "You are the prize."[1] Create a life that matches that truth.

If You Can't See It, You Can't Have It

The beautiful thing about doing the work in the prior chapter around your patterns and addictions is that you can clearly see the basis of how you have operated and functioned in the past. While you may not have a clear idea of what a vision of Deservingness looks like, this work you have done will be invaluable in helping you create this vision.

---

1 Rashawn Renee. *44 Hours & 21 Minutes: A Woman's Truth and Power.* Real Truth International, LLC, 2018.

When you know what you do not want, it becomes a lot easier to create what you do want, even if you have never experienced it before. That is why you need to envision what this new version of you might look like, feel like, and experience because that is the only way you will attain it.

At the beginning, the only version you might be able to see is how your life felt in the past.

From there, you can start putting pieces of the vision together by asking yourself: *What do I want to see in my future?*

Once you have placed these pieces all together, you can create a vision of how your new life will be.

When I finally pulled myself out of that last relationship, I realized I needed to create a vision of what a relationship would look like in which I deserved the best. Since I had never had that kind of relationship in thirty-plus years of relationship experiences, I sat down and took all the pieces, all the thoughts I could bring together of what made me feel less than Deserving in my past relationships, and I simply created the opposite of all of them.

I considered every single experience that made me feel less-than—the knowledge, the feeling, the experience—and I wrote out a vision that was the complete contrast and opposite. I created a relationship where I was valued. My partner was in integrity with me. I was lavished on and treasured, admired, and respected—treated like a queen. The situations I had never experienced in the past became information for the vision I was creating of my new reality.

From Wishing to Believing

I am going to be honest with you. In thirty-something years, I had never experienced what I was writing out as my vision. Looking at my vision, and even having the slightest thought that I might achieve it, seemed at best like a far-fetched wish.

However, I have done enough of this work to know that when you believe something, you will have it. I know you instinctively know that a wish is just a wish, but I needed to move from wishing for reality to bringing myself to the belief it could be mine.

How would I do that?

I took everything I had written in my new vision, everything I had described. I created a scene in which I was in a relationship with someone, and I was living in the experience of everything I had written about. I closed my eyes, and I daydreamed day after day about being in a relationship with someone for which this vision was the experience.

I loved this process so much that sometimes I did not want it to end. Before long, I believed it. It became so real in my imagination that there was no separation between fantasy and reality. At that point, I could believe it was possible for me to have the relationship of my dreams. I could believe it was mine to have because I could see, feel, and experience it. In that vision, I knew it was what I deserved—and that is the key.

Feeding the Dream

You have created your new life, one that reflects what you now think and believe you deserve, and you have created a vision you can believe, see, and feel. The next step is to understand this dream must be fed every day of your life until it becomes your reality. It is like having a baby. The moment a child is born, it is a living, breathing person. However, if a child is not fed daily, they will not continue to grow. They will not reach their full potential. They will not have the joyous life experience they were born to fulfill.

You have given birth to a dream, a new vision of you in a reality where you deserve the best. If you truly want to experience your creation, you will need to feed this dream every day of your life just the same as you would feed a baby. Feed it until it grows and becomes your fulfilled life experience.

Chapter Four

Love and Forgiveness Are Key

CLEAN SLATE

As you begin feeding your vision, there is one thing that can come in like a thief in the night and rob you of your dreams—the hurt and pain of the past. The past can feel heavy and weighted—quite a burden to carry around in life—especially for those of us whose traumatic experiences led us to believe we are not Deserving. The past serves as a constant reminder of that belief. Being able to be free of those beliefs requires starting over—creating a clean slate of the self.

Starting over and creating this blank canvas will take courage. You must be willing to disassociate yourself from the traumas of the past. You must also be willing to not mess up your beautiful new painting of your future by including things you need to forgive yourself for.

You have already done the work to give yourself this new life filled with freedom to choose. Always choose what makes you feel loved and expansive, as if you deserve the best. Minimize adding anything you will need to forgive yourself for.

Access Starting Over

I remember coming back from my trip to Costa Rica after my come-to-Jesus moment where I was told I was experiencing pain and suffering because I did not believe I deserved more. I came back home and realized the only thing that had really changed was I would not be communicating as much with the man who had been the final spoke in my wheel.

However, I was still filled with questions about why this happened: *Why have I allowed this? How could I have caused this to be my reality?*

Blame, shame, anger, and resentment were still present within me, and I was spending a lot of time trying to figure it all out, which only drove me further into pain. Finally, a new thought was introduced in my mind: *What if I could start over?*

What if, instead of trying to answer all these questions, you could have a clean slate, erasing all the past traumatic experiences that led you to believe the level of Deservingness you have?

What if you could begin operating from a life where you are creating new truths that show up as your new reality?

Starting over and creating a new slate is the beautiful gift you give yourself. You have the power, the ability, the right, and everything you need to wipe your past clean and begin again with a blank canvas. That canvas is possible because you no longer hold the traumas of the past.

An End to Suffering

Everything we do in life is driven by the reward we receive. That sounds kind of weird because there are some things we do that create an unpleasant reward, such as suffering. Because of our previous wiring and the fact that we have become addicted to suffering, pain is almost turned into the pleasure response that we seek.

One thing I know for sure: People with Deserving issues suffer. They suffer immensely. My motivation for working to create a clean slate was I wanted to end the suffering I was experiencing. For me, the drive to end that suffering was like air, like oxygen. It became a nonoptional task in my life.

If you are reading this book, you are probably 98 percent committed to ending your suffering. The path to creating your new slate is *forgiveness*. I once read this quote by an unknown author:

I forgive myself for all the things I accepted that
I did not deserve.

If you want to end suffering, the end begins with forgiveness. The first person to forgive is yourself for the choices you made, the situations you accepted, The Lie you believed.

Freedom of Choice

Imagine your life is now a blank canvas, a clean slate. All becomes possible from this point forward. Having made the choice to end suffering, to start over, to forgive yourself—the gift you have given yourself—you now face a choice.

No longer must you live the experiences that are a result of your past. You can, in this moment, create new truths that will create new life experiences. The key is to recognize that the moment you choose to access this blank slate— painting whatever you want to believe about yourself and your life experiences—you receive the gift of choosing what your life looks like: what you believe, what you accept, and what you experience. Freedom is the experience you never had. This freedom is really the ultimate prize, the ultimate reward of doing the work. You are now free to choose what shows up in your life.

Here's a powerful exercise.

Make a list:

- Every violation of your person or space
- Every hurt you experienced
- Every wrong done to you
- Every life-impacting event where you suffered

Be as thorough with this list as you can. Then go back through and forgive each incident.

If this is difficult, think perhaps of times when you have been forgiven or wished to be forgiven. Now, you have the power to grant forgiveness to others. Remember this is about feeling at peace instead of hurting, and is not about letting others off the hook.

I am so grateful for self-forgiveness and God's forgiveness. My creator said to me, "I have forgiven you for what you did and forgive you for everything you will do."

To forgive is to set a prisoner free and discover that the prisoner was you.
~ Louis B. Smedes

Forgive and Forget: Healing the Hurts We Don't Deserve

LEARN TO LOVE EVERYTHING

On this journey of Deservingness and in my commitment to creating this amazing new life experience I deserve, I also found that understanding the power of love is foundational. Love is the highest vibration that exists. It can heal everything.

After enduring enough trauma, enough pain, and enough suffering, reaching for love can be a stretch. Yet, if you want this new life you are choosing, the ability to love everything about your life, including yourself, is key.

Loving You

Self-Love. If I had heard that from another coach or expert one more time as I struggled to regain my life, I think I might have done something illegal. I come to you right now with the notion of self-love as the path to healing and creating this new life of Deservingness, so I understand you might not be too happy with me. I get it. I understand. I have been there.

Yet as much as I resisted, as much as I stomped my feet and raised my fists, when it was all said and done, I took way too long to embrace loving myself. When I finally did, I understood everything. I understood all my past decisions, all the things that I accepted in the past, and all of reasons why no one could truly love me. How could they love me when I couldn't believe in Deserving my own love?

Here is what I realized, and I think you can agree: Within all of us lives a wounded child, one still struggling to make right all the unpleasant experiences and thoughts of ourselves that shaped what we now as adults believe we deserve. The wound in that child can be healed with a simple remedy: *Love.*

It's no coincidence that the year I honored myself the most was also the year I made the most money in our business.

Which is why I would like to share with you the power of loving yourself. Sit with everything you have ever wanted from other people in your life, especially in romantic relationships. What have you sought that has led to you feeling unappreciated, unloved, unfulfilled, or unattended to? As you look at all the relationships in your life and the ways that you sought love, make a list.

That list will be all you need to know about loving yourself. Now it is your turn to learn to give yourself everything you sought in all those relationships. Giving all that love to yourself is a definition of self-love. It is the most profound love you could ever experience.

Have you ever been in love?

Can you remember your desire to show the other person just how much you loved and cared for them?

Have you ever felt like that about yourself? No?

It's time to start.

If you haven't loved yourself enough, imagine becoming more self-loving. It may feel selfish to be so indulgent. I make this promise: Taking care of yourself first will help you demonstrate you love yourself, which, in turn, will make you trust yourself. If you live from a belief that you aren't worthy and don't deserve very much, you also can't trust yourself with your life.

If you want others to believe you deserve the best, you must give it to yourself first. So be *selfish!* As my client and friend Candi Parker once told me, "Feed the self first. After all, you deserve it!"

First Love Yourself, Then Love All Else

How you have experienced Deservingness until this point in your life may have sucked, and my telling you to love yourself is going to land with some possible resistance. Yet, that is the goal. When you are able to review everything in your past that brought you to the place of believing you deserve so little and learn to love that past, you become free, empowered, and able to move forward, to make a different choice.

You need, in essence, to douse the past with love and experience pure forgiveness, fully embracing that it is your life and a part of you. Your past experiences have made you who you are. Love those experiences as you would love your kid who did something to upset you.

Until you are able to feel a deep level of love for everything in your life, the past you have had, the present struggles you are enduring, the fears you have of the future, you will never be free. Until you can blanket it all with love, you will never be able to live out Deserving the best.

What Is Love to You?

Next, let's consider the love you desire from others. My definition of someone loving me was pretty jacked up from the start. Remember my parents in the bedroom and me feeling unloveable? I decided that attention of any kind—good or bad—was love. And to make matters worse, my additional way of defining love came from romance novels, Hallmark movies, and bad relationship experiences of others I had to watch and endure. It never occurred to me that I could define love for myself.

Have you ever thought about your own definition of love?

What is love to you?

Having learned to love yourself—giving yourself all you once looked to others to receive—and having created the ability to love the past, the present, and the future, allows you to become the purest, highest vibration of this energy called *love*.

Define what love looks like for you, both in terms of how you give and share it with others and what it looks like when you receive it.

Can you imagine crafting your own definition so you know this new way you see love is now what you deserve?

ACCESSING A HIGHER POWER

This journey of transforming yourself—from one who has believed your entire life that you deserved very little, to becoming one who now deserves the best—is sometimes going to require an out-of-body, out-of-mind, out-of-your-physical-being partnership with an entity more powerful than you. I will call this entity Source. For me, that is God. On a human level, this transformation of unbelieving something you attached to your entire life will require a strength and courage that is beyond your own capacity. It will require having a connection with a Source more powerful than you.

Yay me! I was a few weeks out of my relationship and in the beginning stages of owning that I deserved way more than I had been accepting. I was 100 percent committed that this was going to be the last time for me; never again would I allow myself to be weak and trapped by past patterns of accepting anything less than the best.

I was fueled by such anger at myself for having allowed my suffering in the first place, that I had an *I-can-do-this* chip on my shoulder all the time. Well, it wasn't long before my ex found his way to my home in the middle of the night and knocked on my bedroom door, asking for us to try again. He was really hard to resist. Seeing a grown man crying and begging was gut-wrenching for me, and for a brief moment, I found myself thinking about how sorry he must be and how hard our new situation must be for him.

Luckily, something deep within reminded me of my commitment to not accepting less than I deserve. That nudge fueled my intuition to know it would be more of the same the second I opened that door. I successfully kept him away that night because something inside kept saying: *Tasha, love yourself more than allowing this to happen again*. I now believe that *something*, that nudge, was God within me.

In the months to follow, there would be many times when my strength would waver. The part of me addicted to our drama would yearn for more. The belief that any attention is better than no attention would fill my mind, and all the weak human parts of me would be so desperate to go back to the familiar Deserving very little.

During these times, I had to rely on a power higher than myself. For me that power was God. I would cry out for help many, many times. Eventually, those cries became fewer and the times between them longer. Without those answered prayers, I shudder to think how I might have gone right back and continued suffering.

This process will require you to believe there is a Source or Power—your Creator, God, the Universe, whatever works for your belief system—that desires only the best for you. Your ability to stay connected to Source and to receive good experiences is tied to your ability to be in relationship with It.

Source wants you to experience true love, joy, abundance and all the best things in life. I do not know about you, but I want to be best friends with the Source from which all good things come. I encourage you to embrace the belief that you were created for a wonderful life. Practice creating the kind of relationship with your

Source where you ask constantly for more of what you want from life and for strength and courage during the times you can't stay strong on your own.

This relationship has been nothing short of life-saving and life-changing for me.

High Vibration

Part of the by-product of a belief in Deserving very little is living in a constant state of low vibration. Suffering, worrying, and being anxious—living out Deserving very little—creates a very low-vibration place from which to experience life. Being committed to transformation will require transitioning to a higher vibration most of the time.

Life is going to happen, and you are going to have moments when you cannot be Pollyanna 100 percent of the time. Our goal is to recognize that the low vibration of Deserving little, suffering, and worrying will only attract more experiences aligned with that energy. In becoming more Deserving, one of the things you must commit to is staying in high vibration as much as possible.

Find activities you enjoy and begin doing them. I had identified with being in this low vibration so much that I would literally seek out time to stay there. I would avoid my friends. I would avoid fun things to do. I would tell myself I need downtime, aka, time to cry, suffer, be anxious, and worry. Ultimately, all I was doing was creating more time to stay in low vibration.

Being in this new state of Deserving the best meant I had to consider what put me in high vibration. At first, it was not a very long list. So, I committed to experiences that would raise my vibration.

When you are deserving very little, you tend to stay away from and avoid people who genuinely love you and want the best for you. This is activity number one. Find a way, redeem yourself, ask for forgiveness, do whatever you need to do to move back into the good graces and appreciation of those people. Make yourself spend time in their presence. Make yourself learn to see what it is like to be in the presence of those who love you as you are. This is one of the easiest ways to grow accustomed to a higher vibration.

Can You Be Grateful?

I mentioned you will be required to have an intimate relationship with a source more powerful than you. You need Source for moments when you are in between your past self—Deserving very little—and the new self you are creating who deserves the best.

Your mind and your ego, so accustomed to a low state, will try to stay in low vibration and convince you to go back over and over again. They will come up with every creative way imaginable to make you stay there. Believe it or not, because you have lived there for so long, there are times when you will actually want to go back. At those times, you need access to a power stronger than you, stronger than your ego, stronger than your comfort zone, stronger than the past-self, the part of you who believed for so long you deserved suffering and believed suffering is normal.

The most effective way to stay connected to this power is to practice gratitude. It is just like loving everything.

Can you be grateful for everything?

As bizarre as it might seem, everything you have endured in your life—pleasant, unpleasant, painful, happy, sad—everything has been part of what led you to the person you are with this now blank slate. It has all informed you. You now know the opposite of what you want.

With this blank slate, you create a magical reality for yourself. So, practice gratitude for everything and try to be in a state of constant gratitude, even when you are sad and crying and confused. Be grateful for something, for being alive, for the ability to cry. I believe people who cannot feel sad enough to cry also cannot experience complete happiness. Even when you are sad and crying, be grateful for the ability.

The ability to express gratitude keeps you connected to this higher power and higher Source. Think of that higher power and higher Source as the story of the footsteps in the sand. In the story, a person sees their life journey as footprints along a beach. At first, two sets of footprints are visible in the sand, indicating that God was walking alongside the person on the journey. Then at one point, there is only one set of prints, not because they were abandoned, but because God or Source carried the person through troubled times. There will be a period where you will need to rely on that Source to carry you.

You can know for sure that Source will carry you when you are in this constant communication with It through gratitude.

The Tests and How to Handle Them

The moment you declare and decide that you will live a life that reflects Deserving the best, you are also pretty much guaranteed your commitment will be tested. It is a fact of the process; it is easier to accept it from the get-go than to be surprised when it shows up in the process.

Let me tell you it is going to come. Here's how to handle it when it does.

As you are going through this process, you will have moments when you feel like the rug has been pulled out from under you. You want to scurry back to the days of being curled up in your room crying all day, being sad and disappointed, your expectations unfulfilled. You will want to go back to that.

As sad as that sounds, it is The Truth. You will be tested in your commitment and your resolve to move toward a life of Deserving the best. And when those days come, I encourage you to pray to whomever and whatever you believe to be your higher source.

I have found myself many an afternoon, midday, early in the morning, walking the beach and full-out bawling like an absolute crazy woman and praying:

> *God and Angels, help me. Help me! I am in a weak moment. I am struggling; I am confused. I do not even know if it is possible to have a life where I deserve the best and it shows up. I do not believe it anymore. I completely declare all my anxiety, all my worries, all my fears, all my struggles – released and removed. I claim this for myself from you, God, my higher Source.*

I have never been let down. Every time I have sought strength, help, and guidance, I have received it. And the tests? They pass, and I move one step closer to my ultimate goal, which is to move away from the life of Deserving very little and stepping into the life of Deserving the best. This is my strongest encouragement for you when the tests come.

Chapter Five

How to Deserve It All

Transformation from lack of Deservingness to Deserving the best is absolutely a journey. It is not for the weary of heart but a journey that is so worth it.

Once you have made the decision to live from a place of Deserving the best, the next major question might be: *How do I do that?*

I know it certainly was for me. I had lived for so long in not Deserving and feeling worthy of so little that making the transition into Deserving more seemed delusional to me. I did not understand what steps to take. My gift to you is sharing what I believe are crucial steps you need to take so you understand how to become Deserving of the best.

THE THREE-STEP DESERVING PROCESS

As I began working on leveling up my Deservingness, I realized I had developed an actual process. Like me, you probably already know it won't ever be enough to just say, *I deserve the best,* and life will say, *Voilà! Here you go*. It won't happen like that. For those words to be true, we need to believe and make life choices that reflect that statement. I describe it as *being transformed*. This is where you become the kind of person who exudes Deserving and receiving the best.

Everything in life follows a system. Transformation absolutely requires steps that, when taken, will create a result. It is like a mathematical formula; it is like science. Do A and you will achieve B. In this section, I will share the process I went through to come out on the other side.

There were three steps:

1. Speaking statements, such as *I deserve the best*
2. Believing those statements to be true
3. Vibrating the energy of Deservingness

If you are reading this book, you are probably well aware of personal development, spirituality, law of attraction, and universal principles. You probably know many steps to manifest the things you want in life.

Have those steps worked so far?

Planting a New Seed

The life experiences we have collected are a reflection of the thoughts, beliefs, and agreements we made in the past. It is as if we planted a seed of Deserving very little throughout our lives, and since then, we have been harvesting fruit from the tree that grew out of those beliefs. The process for changing will be to uproot that tree and plant a new seed.

You have already taken steps to uproot the tree that has been bearing fruit of Deserving very little in your life. You have brought to your awareness The Lie you have accepted, the agreements you have made, and the actions you have taken. You have forgiven yourself and become grateful for all your life experiences. Consider it done. Now the process of living into Deserving the best will require you to take a new seed filled with Deservingness and to plant that seed in your life.

This seed concept might be new and unusual. Yet, its simplicity is what makes it so powerful. Because you never heard it like this before, you will be able to follow this process. I encourage you to plant your seed of Deserving the best and wake up every morning, thinking you have a beautiful plant on your patio that needs your love and attention. Every day, you need to water it, love it, nurture it, and pray over it.

Treat this seed of Deservingness with love. This is the *how* for creating a life of Deserving the best. You must first plant the seed of Deserving the best in your subconscious mind, making this your declaration that you now want to operate from this new belief.

Your Deservingness Tree Flourishes

My past traumatic experiences, especially in relationships, were simply the fruit of the tree I had been picking from. I made the decision to uproot that tree and plant a new seed. The next order of business in my life was to nurture that seed—to pray over it, to fertilize it, water it, ask for blessings on it every day—so I could pick fruit from the tree of Deservingness in my life. The experiences mirrored from that new tree would be the fruit of that tree.

I encourage you to take the simple step of imagining you are planting this new seed of Deserving the absolute best in life in your conscious and subconscious mind, in your heart and your cells, in your spirit and energetic field. Just take a moment and imagine yourself planting that seed inside of you energetically.

And then, imagine that tree of Deserving the best flourishing and thriving, with strong branches, beautiful leaves, and bearing the most delicious and exotic fruit in your life.

What would your life reflect to you?

If you were to pick the fruit of that tree and that fruit became the experiences of Deserving the best showing up in your life, imagine what they might look like and feel like. Now that you have planted this new seed, new experiences will show up in your life. It will be the fruit; your life will bear fruit from this tree of Deservingness.

From this point forward, your absolute priority is to nurture this seed every day.

Those Who Deserve the Best, Desire the Best

I am a powerful manifestor. I once journaled twenty pages about the kind of guy I wanted to manifest, and I attracted a man with 93 to 95 percent of the things I wrote down on those twenty pages. At the time, my Deservingness was so low that even with all those amazing things, I still managed to attract someone who had such brokenness that he mirrored my worthiness issues. Three years of trauma followed, but it taught me how powerful I was.

Having reshaped my life by creating what I stepped into believing, I went back to the drawing board to write about a man who would reflect my new beliefs. He would be a fruit that I would pick from that tree. I played around with this for about a year or so, until one day, I finally had a come-to-Tasha moment where I said to myself: *You have been writing about this new man you want, and you are still not being honest. What do you really want? What is it that you are still not willing to believe you can have?*

By this point, I had many synchronistic experiences of people telling me, "You have not yet attracted the man because you do not believe you can have it all."

I finally decided: *All right, I am willing to go for it. I am willing to ask for what I want and believe I now deserve it all.* I grabbed my journal, and I wrote only two pages. Those two pages finally reflected what my heart truly wanted. And now, I was willing to ask for it.

Within five months of writing those pages, I manifested meeting that man.

Having planted this seed, you are now directing God and the Universe to bear the fruit of your tree. At this moment, you have the power within you to say what kind of fruit you truly want from this tree.

Are you willing to acknowledge and ask for what you really want?

WRITE YOURSELF INTO BELIEVING

I have proven the power of pen and paper, black and white, seeing physically in words the thoughts I want my subconscious mind to embrace. I am excited to share with you the ease of believing a new thought by simply writing it and introducing it to your subconscious mind, which will do the remainder of the work for you.

New Beliefs

You become what you believe – not what you
wish or want, but what you truly believe.
Wherever you are in life, look at your beliefs.
They put you there.

~ Oprah

As you continue on this journey of Deservingness, your success will be a reflection of what you choose to believe. I hope you have now embraced a life of believing you deserve the best.

How do you get your mind to agree, to say yes to these beliefs?

Sit down with pen and paper, and ask: *What do I want to believe I deserve?*

Answer in terms of what you deserve in life, not what was told to you—not what society, your parents, or your friends want. You have let that go. It is all gone; all that is gone. You are in the driver seat. You choose what you want to believe.

Write it with pen and paper.

Here are some suggestions:

- *I believe I deserve the best.*
- *I believe life shows me every day that I deserve the best.*
- *I believe every person who enters my life reflects this new belief.*
- *Every experience I have is a mirror of this powerful belief within me.*
- *I believe others receive my best, and I deserve to receive their best.*

Add anything else you now choose to believe you deserve. Write it all out.

Put It in Writing

Now that you have written out—for yourself to see—the new beliefs you are choosing to live by, we will create, in writing, a moment in time where you experience this new belief. You will create a scene that reflects this belief.

I will give you an example. I wanted to believe I deserved to experience the fittest, healthiest, sexiest body I could achieve. One approach would be to create a weight loss plan, to make an exercise commitment. The reason I never achieved that result before was I never believed I could do it, or that I deserved to have that body. In fact, I had some trauma in my past that said that whenever I looked sexy, I misused my sensuality.

I needed to eradicate all those old beliefs. I wrote myself a new belief, and then I wrote a scene in which someone else was telling me how amazing I looked, asking me what I had done. In this scene, I shared with them that it was not about dieting or exercising or any of those things, but I had simply stepped into Deserving my best and loving myself.

Four months later, on a girls' night out with my friends, I found myself living it with my best friend saying, "Wow, I have never seen you look so sexy. You look amazing! I have never seen you dress like this. What are you doing?" And there I was, in the manifestation of my dreams, in the manifestation of what I had written.

Think of an area in your life in which you want to see this new Deservingness belief reflected. Create a scene in which you are in a conversation and this belief is being mirrored back to you clearly, and someone outside of you is commenting, asking, or suggesting. Imagine you have now achieved this level of Deservingness. Put it in writing as if it has already happened.

Simply give yourself an extra dose of love. It will pass; I promise.

STAND FOR THE BEST

Your biggest advocate, cheerleader, and support team on this journey will and must be you. It is you who will need to love yourself more than enough, to be willing to stand for receiving the best. The Universe will simply bring and give to you what you are willing to accept.

Let's say you decide you deserve to move to new living accommodations as part of your new Deservingness beliefs. You make a list of ten *must-haves* for the new space to satisfy this desire. When you stand for yourself, you decide unequivocally to only accept places that meet nine of ten of the requirements on your list.

If you ask for ten out of ten and receive a six out of ten and accept it, the Universe will stop. But if you receive a six and say: *This is not enough,* the Universe will continue to give you a seven, then an eight, then a nine, and finally a ten. You need to be in receiving mode and to stand for what you believe is the best for you.

You deserve the best. Create a life that mirrors that belief. Live experiences that show you every day and in every way that you are Deserving of it all.

You Decide

This is where the fun—*total sarcasm*—begins. The play of energy might look like this: You decided you want the best—okay. However, for so long you have accepted so little. Let's say you have accepted in all areas of life a two to three out of ten. And now you have made the big proclamation, you are taking a stand for yourself, saying you deserve the best. Well, the next thing you know, life might bring you a four in one or all areas of your life.

Sure, it is movement; it is better than what you have been accustomed to. You must look at it and decide if it is what you deserve.

On those days when you receive two or three of the items on your new Deservingness list, it's not because the Universe wants to test you—it is simply part of the process, giving you the opportunity to stand for the best. Each opportunity presents a decision, a choice: *Is this my new best? Is this my new level of Deservingness*?

The beauty of this process is that, in every instance, you are the one who decides. You choose yes or no. For so long, you have accepted so little that seeing a four or a five might appear as a beautiful, shiny object. However, taking a stand for a ten will require you to always stand for a ten. It is okay to accept an eight or a nine, but most definitely not a four or a five.

Once I made this decision, I started seeing the four, five, and six show up. I became really excited. Then the Universe was so benevolent it took these seemingly *better numbers* away from me, it pulled them back because it knew how powerfully I wanted to stand for a ten. And when it pulled them away and things did not work out, it hurt.

I thought: *This is not worth it. I want to go back to my three because at least I have something.*

I took myself back to the process of writing out why I believed I deserved the best. I gave myself the time to allow it to pass. And then, I saw the benevolence and the love of God and the Universe in taking away the fours, fives, and sixes from me—reminding me I am the one who decides.

I can always decide to wait for a ten. Just like you can. Wait for your ten.

Be Relentless in Your Pursuit

I say this with all the love in my heart for you because I know the love that you need right now. I remember the love I needed. People who live long lives of Deserving very little have become so accustomed to accepting just that—very little. As you move forward on this journey, you will receive a little more on each step than you have been accustomed to for a long time.

I encourage you to commit. Think of this journey as the Olympics. You are not going for silver, you are not going for bronze, you are always going for gold.

Go for gold!

During my divorce process, my mentor Fran Asaro asked me to choose my ideal way of speaking up for myself as we negotiated what was fair to me in the sharing of our assets. In the past, I had accepted things because of my fears and Deservingness issues, and I tended to settle for whatever was offered to avoid any conflict. My mentor shared this Olympics concept and said I was always choosing the silver medal for myself by choosing what reflected Deserving little. She encouraged me to *go for gold* in every conversation, to stand for Deserving the best by asking for what I wanted, and to reward myself with the gold medal by standing fully for myself.

The difference between bronze and gold, sometimes, will be your decision to pursue the best. Because this new paradigm, this new way of living, is you, saying: *I am not stopping until I begin to pick from my tree of Deservingness. I am pursuing the best in every area of my life. I am going all the way, for gold. I deserve the best.*

The Truth You Never Knew

I have such gratitude for the benevolence of God, Source, the Universe in my life. *The Science of Getting Rich* (Wattles, 1910) says, "Nature is friendly to your plans; it wants you to have your desires even more than you want it." That thought brings tears to my eyes.

Even more than I want what is best for me, God wants what is best for me. How can I not love a Source that wants complete abundance, love, joy, peace, and ease for me, even at the times when I have not believed I deserved them? I have come to appreciate that knowledge because there are many times when I have gone off course, off track, back to my old ways, and have been redirected, sometimes not so gently, but always with love.

I see that clearly now.

At this point, having shared everything I know to share with you, this will be my final word of encouragement. As you go through these experiences, the ups and downs of this journey, I promise you three things:

1. If you follow the process, you will arrive at a new day in your life when you begin to reap the fruit from your tree of Deservingness. You will be amazed at how life is suddenly responding and bringing you the best because that is what you now believe you deserve.

2. You will experience a profound gratitude when you see The Truth that God loves you, has always loved you, and has always wanted the best for you. The Source of all creation created you in truth, created you to live a life Deserving the best.

3. There is nothing you need to do to *prove* you deserve the best. You were created to receive it; it is your birthright.

Now, it is your turn to say yes.

Conclusion

I am deserving. I deserve all good. Not some, not a little bit, but all good. I now move past all negative, restricting thoughts. I release and let go of the limitations of my parents. I love them, and I go beyond them. I am not their negative opinions, nor their limiting beliefs. I am not bound by any of the fears or prejudices of the current society I live in. I no longer identify with limitation of any kind.

In my mind, I have total freedom. I now move into a new space of consciousness, where I am willing to see myself differently. I am willing to create new thoughts about myself and about my life. My new thinking becomes new experiences.

I now know and affirm that I am at one with the Prospering Power of the Universe. As such, I now prosper in a number of ways. The totality of possibilities lies before me. I deserve life, a good life. I deserve love, an abundance of love. I deserve good health. I deserve to live comfortably and to prosper. I deserve joy and happiness. I deserve freedom to be all that I can be. I deserve more than that. I deserve all good.

> *The Universe is more than willing to manifest my new beliefs. And I accept this abundant life with joy, pleasure, and gratitude. For I am deserving. I accept it; I know it to be true.*
>
> Louise L. Hay
>
> *Love Yourself, Heal Your Life Workbook*[2]

This journey to Deserving the best is not for the fainthearted. However, the reward is like nothing you have ever imagined. Being able to hold your head high, look yourself in the mirror, and stand in the presence of others with the knowingness of who you are and what you are claiming as your own will become the most ecstatic personal experience you have ever had. It will be the best gift you have ever given to yourself.

At times, the journey might feel a little treacherous. It might; that is just The Truth.

Would you do it over and over again to become free, to be filled with your own love, and to live a life that mirrors back to you that you now believe you deserve the best?

I do not know about you, but I would do it all over again, a hundred times, to get back to this place of living from Deserving the best.

---

2 Louise Hay. *Love Yourself, Heal Your Life Workbook*. Hay House, 1990.

Dealing With Bad Days

I share a word of caution and a lot of love in this section. Be gentle with yourself. This process requires undoing years of beliefs and actions, breaking patterns of behaviors so deep and so subconscious they have become habitual. Yes, I am really excited for you. I am with you, now that you are stepping into this new life experience that mirrors all that you truly deserve.

However, I would be remiss if I did not caution you that there will be days—there will be moments, there will be experiences—when the pull to go back is so strong it feels like an effort or a struggle to resist. Here is how you deal with that. On those days when it seems so hard to move forward, it seems so challenging to stand for what you now deserve, grab your pen and paper, recommit, write out again why this new life, this new way of being, is what you want so much.

Remember you want it more than you want to go back to the pain, the trauma, and the hurt of a life constantly in turmoil. Grab your pen and paper and make yourself see why you want this new life. On those days, you do not need to move the mountain. There is no big thing you need to do other than to write out, again, why this is what you want—why you deserve the best.

You planted a seed of Deservingness recently, and it needs your love, your care, your attention, your nurturing. This new life you crave will manifest in direct proportion to the amount of time and effort you personally give to nurturing the seed of Deservingness within you. It is perhaps the most important job you need to do for the next few months to come.

Remember to think of this life as a seed sprouting into a beautiful new plant and then ultimately into a tree with branches and fruit. The fruit of that tree will be new experiences in your life. Wake up every day and in your quiet time, ask God, Source, Universe, the heavens, or your angels to help you pour heavenly blessings on this tree. Then give it your nurturing attention so that it continues to grow and bear the new fruit you are creating in your life.

Do not forget there are days that feel like you are being tested. They will—not might—they will occur. Be armed and ready. Remember your new belief statement, your new truth, and commit to going to war against your old self by declaring your new beliefs, your new truth, your new reasons why you are going for this new life.

As it says in *The Alchemist* by Paolo Coelho:

> Before a dream is realized, the soul of the world tests everything that was learned along the way. It does this not because it is evil, but so that we can, in addition to realizing our dreams, master the lessons we have learned as we have moved

> toward the dream. That is the point at which most people give up. It is the point at which we say, in the language of the desert, one dies of thirst just when the palm trees have appeared on the horizon.[3]

Remember, the palm trees are just on the horizon.

---

3 Coelho, Paolo. *The Alchemist*. Alan R. Clarke, trans. Harper Collins: New York, 1993.

Next Steps

Check out the Deservingness Podcast featured on

Tashachen.com

To find out more, visit these websites:

TashaChen.com

ScienceofGettingRichAcademy.com

Or contact me via email at: tasha@tashachen.com.

About the Author

Tasha Chen is a Master Money Manifesting Mentor and co-founder of the Science of Getting Rich Academy.

As a seasoned entrepreneur and business mentor, Tasha noticed there was one singular distinction between those who succeeded in their lives and those who did not. As fate would have it, she learned this lesson through a traumatic personal experience that had her examine her *Worthiness* and how it limited her own success in many areas of her life. Tasha now passionately shares that *Deservingness* is the single most powerful factor in determining the way we experience life.

Tasha Chen's impactful manifestation and mindset philosophy has helped friends, family, colleagues, and many entrepreneurs around the globe shift their perspective on money and their personal stories around Deservingness as it relates to abundance. Beyond delivering access to the freedom of financial abundance, Tasha has helped business owners shift from struggling to reconnecting with their heart's dream, stepping into their power, and remembering how to create their reality with a process that proves to be fun and easy.

She attended Nova Southeastern University and has bachelor of science in Banking and Finance and a master's degree in International Business and Banking.

Tasha's work, delivered through international speaking events and workshops, as well as via online media, has impacted the lives of thousands of people, guiding them to create well over $45,000,000 in new income.

Tasha resides in a quiet seaside town in Florida with her son.

Made in the USA
Las Vegas, NV
20 December 2021